# ADD MORE BABES!

## Awesome BIG NATE™ Comics

## by LINCOLN PEIRCE

**TOPPER BOOKS**
AN IMPRINT OF PHAROS BOOKS
A SCRIPPS HOWARD COMPANY
NEW YORK

First published in 1992.

BIG NATE ™ comic strips: © 1991, 1992 United Feature Syndicate, Inc.

Library of Congress Cataloging-in-Publication Data
Peirce, Lincoln.
[Big Nate. Selections.]
Add more babes! : awesome BIG NATE comics/by Lincoln Peirce.
p. cm.
ISBN 0-88687-682-6 (pbk.) : $7.95
I. Title.  II. Title: Big Nate.
PN6728.B49P45    1992
91-41234    741.5'973 — dc20    CIP

Printed in the United States of America

Topper Books
An Imprint of Pharos Books
A Scripps Howard Company
200 Park Avenue
New York, NY 10166

10 9 8 7 6 5 4 3 2 1

FIRST DAY OF
# SCHOOL!

I do not believe this day is here already. I practically just finished school, and now it's time to go back.

September [Dang!]

**3**

This stinks. I hate school. This is the worst day in the history of my life. But does **DAD** see that? I think **NOT!**

Let's GO, sleepy-head!

Shake! Shake!

You can tell he doesn't see that this is the worst day of the year. He is so clueless. You can tell that to him today is just another day.

© 1991 United Feature Syndicate, Inc.

YES!

---

HEY HEY **HEY!**

WOW! WHAT'S ALL THAT STUFF?

SCHO
BU

MY DAD BOUGHT ME SOME SCHOOL SUPPLIES! HE WANTS ME TO BE PREPARED FOR THE YEAR!

DANG!

BINDERS! A SIX-POCKET ORGANIZER! A NOTEPAD! A RULER! A COMPASS! A PENCIL CASE!

© 1991 United Feature Syndicate, Inc.

MAN! YOU'RE **LOADED!**

I KNOW! FINALLY I HAVE SOMETHING I CAN TRADE FOR A DECENT LUNCH!

---

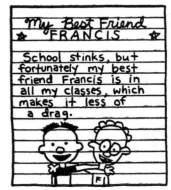

My Best Friend
★ FRANCIS ★

School stinks, but fortunately my best friend Francis is in all my classes, which makes it less of a drag.

We always make sure we are sitting next to each other in class, so then we can mess around and pass notes and stuff.

Field goal!

Dang!

FLICK!

Also, I was originally assigned to share a locker with Sally Wilson, but I booted her out so my best friend Francis could move in.

KICK!

© 1991 United Feature Syndicate, Inc.

DID YOU NOTICE I USED THE WORDS "BEST FRIEND" **THREE** TIMES?

FOR THE LAST TIME, I AM **NOT** GOING TO LET YOU COPY MY MATH HOMEWORK!

---

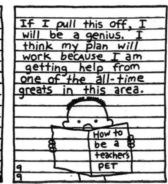

# HOMEWORK!

The school year has barely started, and already Mrs. Godfrey is going crazy with the homework assignments.

SUMMER VACATION IS OVER, people! WA HA HA HA HAAAA!

What a sadist. Today she assigned us three chapters to read and a whole bunch of questions to answer.

THUD! POINK!

So now I am sitting here at home and there is no way I am ever going to finish this stuff. In situations like this there is only one thing to do.

HELLO, FRANCIS?

WHAT DO YOU WANT?

FRANCIS, DID YOU DO THE SOCIAL STUDIES HOMEWORK?

YEAH, I DID IT.

WELL, GIVE ME THE ANSWERS! I CAN'T FIGURE THIS STUFF OUT!

I'M NOT GOING TO JUST GIVE YOU THE ANSWERS!

WHY NOT?

BECAUSE IT WOULD BE WRONG! YOU WON'T LEARN ANYTHING IF I DO ALL THE WORK FOR YOU!

I'VE GOT TO FIND A BEST FRIEND WITH A LESS RIGOROUS MORAL CODE....

# Detention!

Well, I got in trouble. Francis would not give me the answers for the Social Studies homework, so of course I had nothing to hand in.

PLEASE?! NO.

icicles

Naturally Godfrey threw a hairy and gave me detention. Right now I am sitting in the detention room. I have to sit here for a whole hour.

Detention Room

BOOT!

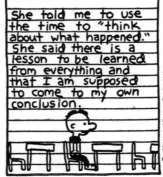

She told me to use the time to "think about what happened." She said there is a lesson to be learned from everything and that I am supposed to come to my own conclusion.

THIS IS ALL FRANCIS' FAULT.

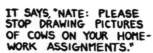

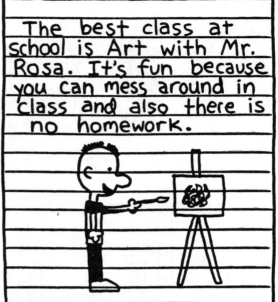

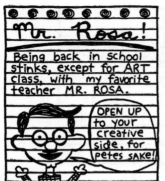

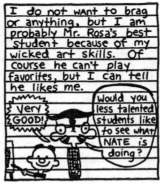

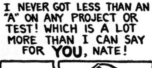

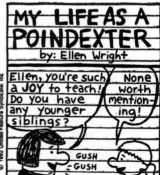

**Awesome BIG NATE comics**

**The Adventures of Dr. CESSPOOL!**
★★★★★★★★★
a comic by NATE WRIGHT

Doctor! What are you doing?

Performing a brain transplant, of course! Otherwise this poor devil hasn't got a chance!!

But this man isn't even a patient! He's our janitor!

Hmmm. No wonder he put up such a struggle! Oh well... NEXT PATIENT!

Sorry to keep you waiting!

That's OK, Doc!

It's nice of you to leave this bowl of potato chips in your waiting room!

Potato chips?

Munch! Munch!

E-GAD! MY SCAB collection!

IF MY ART CAREER DOESN'T WORK OUT, DO YOU THINK I HAVE A FUTURE IN MEDICINE?

I THINK YOU MAY SPEND A LOT OF TIME IN HOSPITALS, YES...

YOU'RE IN LUCK, MR. ROSA! I JUST FINISHED THE LATEST INSTALLMENT OF "DR. CESSPOOL COMICS"!

"DR. CESSPOOL"?

HE'S MY OWN COMIC CREATION! HERE, TAKE A LOOK!

"READ DR. CESSPOOL'S ZANY ADVENTURES IN A HOSPITAL EMERGENCY ROOM AS HE TRIES TO COMBINE HIS DUAL LOVES IN ONE EXCITING CAREER!"

"DUAL LOVES?"

MEDICINE AND LUMBERJACKING! HE'S A REAL RENAISSANCE MAN!

MR. ROSA DIDN'T LIKE MY "DR. CESSPOOL COMICS," DAD...

HE DIDN'T, EH?

NO. SEE THIS LAST PANEL WHERE DR. CESSPOOL IS AMPUTATING THIS PATIENT'S HAND?

UH... YES.

MR. ROSA SAID THAT WAS TOO VIOLENT! CAN YOU BELIEVE THAT?

HMM...

PERHAPS DR. CESSPOOL SHOULDN'T BE SCREAMING "YAHOO..."

THE MAN LOVES HIS WORK! IS THAT A CRIME?

LOOK! THIS BULLETIN SAYS MRS. GODFREY'S GOING TO BE OUT ALL WEEK!

IT SAYS SHE'S HAVING MINOR SURGERY.

YEAH, I HEARD SHE HAS AN INGROWN TOENAIL...

AN INGROWN TOENAIL? THAT'S JUST WHAT THEY **WANT** US TO THINK! I'M SURE IT'S SOMETHING MUCH MORE INTERESTING!

LIKE WHAT?

DR. CESSPOOL'S PLASTIC SURGERY HUT

I want a new face, Doctor! Mine keeps scaring my students!

Hey, I can see WHY!

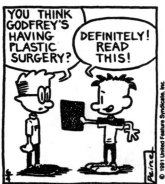

YOU THINK GODFREY'S HAVING PLASTIC SURGERY?

DEFINITELY! READ THIS!

DR. CESSPOOL'S PLASTIC SURGERY HUT

I want a whole new face, Doctor! A whole new identity!

You've come to the right place!

The FIRST step is to get rid of the face you've got NOW!

NURSE! My belt sander!

Yes, Doctor!

continued!

DR. CESSPOOL'S PLASTIC SURGERY HUT

Step One of your plastic surgery is complete, Mrs. Godfrey! I've erased your face!

Now for step Two! Like a great artist, I will create a masterpiece on this blank canvas!

NURSE! My crayons!!

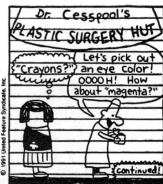

Dr. Cesspool's PLASTIC SURGERY HUT

"Crayons?"

Let's pick out an eye color! OOOOH! How about "magenta?"

continued!

21

**Awesome BIG NATE comics**

**ADD MORE BABES!**

**Awesome BIG NATE comics**

**ADD MORE BABES!**

**ADD MORE BABES!**

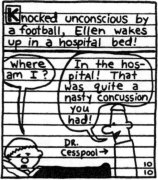

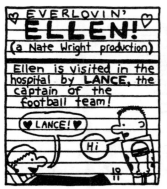

29

31

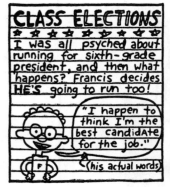

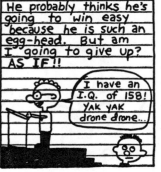

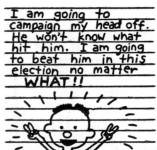

**ADD MORE BABES!**

WHAT ARE YOU WORKING ON?

I GOT IN TROUBLE FOR MY FIRST BATCH OF CAMPAIGN POSTERS, SO I'M MAKING NEW ONES.

THEY SEEM A LITTLE BORING, THOUGH...

VOTE FOR NATE

THAT'S BECAUSE YOU'RE NOT TELLING THE VOTERS WHO YOU ARE! YOU NEED TO IDENTIFY YOURSELF!

WHAT DO YOU MEAN?

"VOTE FOR NATE: ELLEN'S BROTHER!"

HOO BOY...

WHAT'S THAT?

NOT THAT IT'S ANY OF YOUR BEESWAX, BUT IT'S THE CAMPAIGN SPEECH I'M GIVING TO THE STUDENT BODY!

YEAH, I'VE GOT ONE TOO! I'VE BEEN WORKING ON IT ALL WEEK!

I'VE DEVELOPED A 10-POINT PLAN TO RADICALLY REVISE OUR STUDENT COUNCIL, RE-STRUCTURE THE 6TH GRADE SOCIAL EVENTS COMMITTEE, AND ESTABLISH A STUDENT JUDICIAL BOARD!

RIP!

DID YOU FINISH COUNTING THE VOTES, MR. ROSA?

YUP! THE RESULTS ARE IN!

CLASS ELECTION TODAY

WELL, WHO WON? HIM OR ME?

NEITHER ONE OF YOU! THE WINNER WAS SHEILA STAPLETON!

WELL, I'M SURE I FINISHED A CLOSE SECOND!

I DIDN'T EVEN KNOW ANYBODY ELSE WAS RUNNING!

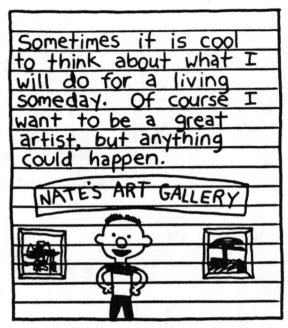

Sometimes it is cool to think about what I will do for a living someday. Of course I want to be a great artist, but anything could happen.

NATE'S ART GALLERY

Fifty years from now I could be a movie star. Fifty years from now I could be a famous writer. Fifty years from now I could be President!

Mr. President!

Mr. President!

CLICK!

Fifty years from now, I could still be waiting for the bathroom.

Hurry UP!

La LA La.... I am so beautiful...

You can always tell when Dad is down in the dumps because he sits around listening to all his old records.

How this music is supposed to improve his mood is a mystery. How depressing can you GET?

Sigh

La LA LA Eve of Destruction... Hum de dum..

7/19

Of course you can't tell Dad that. If you make any comments about his music, he throws a hairy.

WILL YOU **STOP** MAKING TORNADO NOISES DURING "BLOWIN' IN THE WIND"?!

**ADD MORE BABES!**

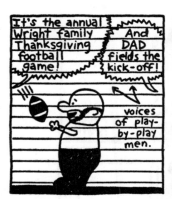

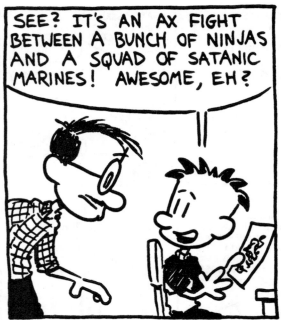

ADD MORE BABES!

**Awesome BIG NATE comics**

**Panel 1:** WELL, MR. ROSA, I'VE CHOSEN A SUBJECT FOR MY ART REPORT!

**Panel 2:** I'M GOING TO WRITE A REPORT ABOUT ONE OF THE GREATEST ARTISTS OF **ALL TIME**!

GREAT!

**Panel 3:** WHO IS IT? MICHELANGELO? REMBRANDT? VAN GOGH?

RUSTY SIENNA, STAR OF "OIL PAINTING WITH RUSTY"!

**Panel 4:** I SHOULD HAVE SEEN THIS COMING...

WHO ARE THOSE OTHER GUYS YOU MENTIONED?

**Panel 5:** I WENT TO THE LIBRARY LIKE YOU SAID, MR. ROSA!

**Panel 6:** I COULDN'T FIND A SINGLE BOOK ABOUT RUSTY SIENNA!

REALLY...

**Panel 7:** OUR LIBRARY STINKS! I LOOKED THROUGH EVERY SINGLE BOOK IN THE "OLD MASTERS" SECTION!

**Panel 8:** I'M NOT SURE RUSTY QUALIFIES AS AN "OLD MASTER"...

SURE HE DOES! THE MAN'S **FORTY** IF HE'S A **DAY**!

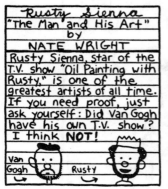

**Panel 9:**
Rusty Sienna
"The Man and His Art"
by
NATE WRIGHT
Rusty Sienna, star of the T.V. show "Oil Painting with Rusty," is one of the greatest artists of all time. If you need proof, just ask yourself: Did Van Gogh have his own T.V. show? I think **NOT**!

Van Gogh          Rusty

**Panel 10:**
Born in Sandusky, Ohio as "Joe Smith," Rusty realized that he needed an artsy name if he was to become a master painter. He changed his name to "Rory Umber" but it didn't work out.

Starving Artist SALE

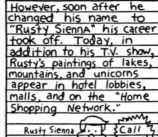

**Panel 11:**
However, soon after he changed his name to "Rusty Sienna" his career took off. Today, in addition to his T.V. show, Rusty's paintings of lakes, mountains, and unicorns appear in hotel lobbies, malls, and on the "Home Shopping Network."

Rusty Sienna ORIGINALS
$19.95
Call NOW!

**Panel 12:** LIKE AN AUTO ACCIDENT, THIS IS SICKLY COMPELLING...

AND THEY SAY THERE ARE NO MORE HEROES!

GUESS WHAT, MR. ROSA? I JUST JOINED THE SCHOOL NEWSPAPER!

GREAT! CONGRATULATIONS, NATE!

YUP! MY FIRST ASSIGNMENT IS TO WRITE AN ARTICLE ABOUT ONE OF THE TEACHERS, AND I CHOSE YOU!

WELL, I'M FLATTERED!

BUT I'LL WARN YOU: IT MAY NOT BE VERY INTERESTING! I LEAD A PRETTY QUIET, UNEVENTFUL EXISTENCE!

"MY LIFE IS MEANINGLESS," SAYS FRUSTRATED ARTIST...

NOW, WHERE SHALL I BEGIN?

---

Notes for article on:
MR. ROSA
by:
Nate "Scoop" Wright

- Was born in small town in Midwest
- Did first crayon drawing at age 3.
- Got first paint set at age 6

NATE
Nate
NATE

- First visit to Art Museum
TURNING POINT IN HIS LIFE!!

- In high school did first oil painting

what a GRAB!

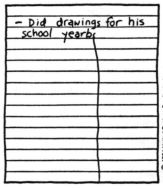

- Did drawings for his school yearb

...THEN, IN MY SECOND YEAR OF COLLEGE...

ZZZZ...

---

**MR. ROSA, SCHOOL ART TEACHER**
by
Nate "Scoop" Wright

Mr. Rosa, the sixth grade art teacher, has taught here at P.S. 38 for nine years. He is also the faculty advisor of the school chess team.

Illustrations by:
Nate "Scoop" Wright

In his spare time, Mr. Rosa does his own paintings. He calls them "abstract," which means that no one likes them. When asked if he has ever sold a painting, Mr. Rosa responded, "no comment."

SPLASH!

Although Mr. Rosa is a bachelor, unnamed sources report that he has been seen down at the local "Pizza Hut" with Miss Burton, the school nurse. They may be an item.

Next week: Up close and personal with Mr. Jenkins, the school janitor.

THEY DON'T CALL ME "SCOOP" FOR NOTHING!

**Awesome BIG NATE comics**

# FRANCIS

Considering the fact that we are best friends, Francis and I are pretty different.

Francis→    ←Me

For example: He is sort of a brain. He gets good grades in everything and all the teachers practically want to adopt him.

VERY good Francis!!

PAT pat

May I have EXTRA homework please?

Sometimes I wonder how the two of us ever got to be friends in the first place.

I'VE WONDERED THE SAME THING....

FRANCIS! LOOK! FRANCIS!

Peirce

# HOMEWORK!

As usual, Mrs. Godfrey assigned a ton of homework, which I didn't finish since I am not the wicked brain you have to be to pass her class.

Come **ON**, people!

CLAP
CLAP

Pass in those home-works NOW!

Of course if I tell **HER** that, she throws a hairy. But when she came around and asked for my homework, I had to say SOMEthing.

Um... I left it in my locker.

WELL, SUPPOSE WE GO TO YOUR LOCKER TOGETHER AND **GET** IT, HMMM?

That was when my day started going downhill.

Dang!

Peirce

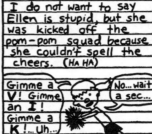

☆ ★ ☆ ★ ☆ ★ ☆
The Zany Escapades of
**ELLEN!**

Ellen, a bleached-blonde high school sophomore, is 15. By a wacky coincidence, this is also her I.Q.

Duh.

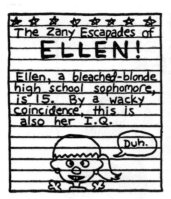

I do not want to say Ellen is stupid, but she was kicked off the pom-pom squad because she couldn't spell the cheers. (HA HA)

Gimme a V! Gimme an I! Gimme a K!...Uh...

No...wait a sec...

Trip!

Yes, folks, it is hard to believe that a creature like Ellen comes from the same gene pool as her brilliant and witty future-artist brother, NATE!

Dang! More acne!

Draw Draw

I'LL KILL HIM....

UH OH...

"THE ZANY ESCAPADES OF ELLEN?" WHO TOLD YOU YOU COULD MAKE A COMIC STRIP ABOUT ME?

WHO SAYS IT'S ABOUT YOU?

HOW MANY **OTHER** HIGH SCHOOL SOPHOMORES NAMED ELLEN DO YOU KNOW?

HEY, I'M SURE THERE ARE **THOUSANDS!**

OH YEAH? AND HOW MANY OF THOSE THOUSANDS HAVE A "BRILLIANT AND WITTY FUTURE-ARTIST BROTHER NAMED NATE?"

STOP IT! YOU'RE MAKING ME **BLUSH!**

**BLUSH?** I'M GONNA MAKE YOU **BLEED!**

I DON'T APPRECIATE BEING RIDICULED IN YOUR STUPID COMIC STRIP, NATE! GET RID OF IT!

FINE!

I'LL ERASE YOU!

GOODBYE, ELLEN...GOODBYE FOREVER... LA TA TA TEE TA.... HUM DIDDLY DUM...

ERASE ERASE

SAY! THIS IS EVEN MORE FUN THAN DRAWING YOU!

**JUST DO IT!**

WHAT ARE YOU DRAWING?

I'M GOING TO CREATE A NEW INSTALLMENT OF "DR. CESSPOOL COMICS"...

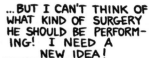
...BUT I CAN'T THINK OF WHAT KIND OF SURGERY HE SHOULD BE PERFORMING! I NEED A NEW IDEA!

DR. CESSPOOL'S **HOUSE O' HAIR!**

Welcome! What kind of hair would you like?

I was thinking of something kind of William Shatner-ish!

DR. CESSPOOL'S **HOUSE O' HAIR!**

This *is* called the "hair-by-hair" method! I attach new hairs to your scalp one-by-one!

Sounds good, Doc!

NURSE! My staple gun!

STAPLE GUN??

WAIT a minute! Aren't you going to give me an anaesthetic?

Hmmm.. Maybe that WOULD be a good idea.

NURSE! Rub an ice cube on this man's head!

Yes, Doctor!

HOW COME THESE DUMB COMICS OF YOURS NEVER HAVE ANY FEMALE CHARACTERS?

I HAVE A FEMALE CHARACTER! DOCTOR CESSPOOL'S FAITHFUL NURSE!

BIG WHOOP! SHE DOESN'T EVEN HAVE A **NAME**!

**SURE** SHE DOES! READ THE LAST PANEL!

DON'T MISS the next adventure ✩ ✩ ✩ OF: ✩ ✩

DR. CESSPOOL and his faithful nurse, **MAUREEN BIOLOGY!**

OH, BROTHER...

I BELIEVE YOU OWE ME AN APOLOGY!

# CHRISTMAS

is less than 2 weeks away!

HO HO **HO!**

AWESOME! Christmas is my favorite holiday.

The best part about Christmas is all the presents. I am trying to figure out what Dad got me, but he is being wicked sneaky. He has done a good job of hiding stuff.

Tippy-toe
Tippy-
    toe

But I am not giving up. Somewhere in this house he is hiding my Christmas presents, and I am going to keep looking until I find them.

?  ?

12
12

JUST BROWSING?

ER.... HI, DAD.

Christmas Vacation
BOOK REPORT

"MOBY DICK"

My book report is on "Moby Dick." The book is called that because that is the name of the main character: a whale named Moby Dick.

While Moby is swimming around the ocean, minding his own business, he is being chased by Captain Ahab, a one-legged sailor who is totally crazed and wants to kill poor Moby. Why, you ask? That is what Moby would like to know.

AVAST!

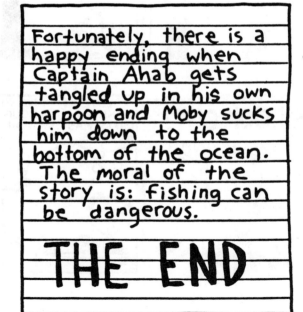

Fortunately, there is a happy ending when Captain Ahab gets tangled up in his own harpoon and Moby sucks him down to the bottom of the ocean. The moral of the story is: fishing can be dangerous.

THE END

DONE!

JUST IN TIME... HERE COMES THE BUS.

1/7/92

**ADD MORE BABES!**

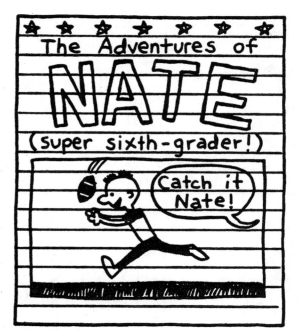

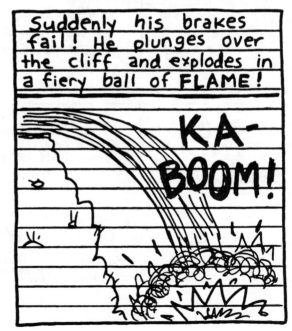

**ADD MORE BABES!**

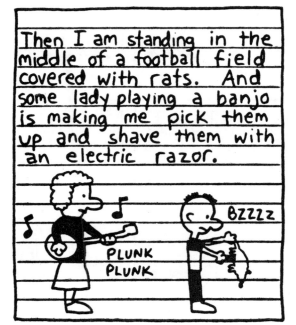

♪ SCHOOL **DANCE!** ♪

The first dance of the year is tonight! The school gym is getting all decorated and there is going to be a D.J. and stuff.

ROCK the HOUSE! (Note how he looks nothing like his radio voice.)

I have never been to a dance before. So of course I am pretty psyched. But not as psyched as Dad.

A dance? Really?

For some reason he is really into this being my first dance. I don't know what the big deal is, but he is totally out of control.

You know, I used to be quite a dancer myself!

WANT ME TO SHOW YOU HOW TO DO "THE HUSTLE"?

GET REAL, DAD.

WOW! OUR FIRST DANCE!

I KNOW! THIS IS WICKED!

AS SOON AS WE WALK OUT ON THAT DANCE FLOOR, WE'RE NOT KIDS ANYMORE!

YOU SAID IT!

THIS IS THE NIGHT WE BECOME **MEN!**

RIGHT!

YOU FIRST.

NO, **YOU** FIRST!

◎ AT THE ◎ *Dance!*

It is kind of weird being at a dance and seeing all the girls that you see in school every day. At a dance they act kind of different.

(they travel in packs)

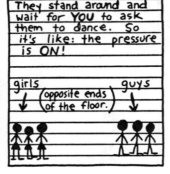

They stand around and wait for **YOU** to ask them to dance. So it's like: the pressure is ON!

girls          guys
↓ (opposite ends ↓
   of the floor.)

But it is important not to rush into anything. You have to be cool and take your time. Fortunately, being cool is my specialty.

WE'VE BEEN SITTING HERE FOR TWO HOURS. MAYBE WE SHOULD MAKE OUR MOVE.

UH..... I DON'T LIKE THIS SONG! LET'S WAIT FOR A GOOD SONG!

**ADD MORE BABES!**

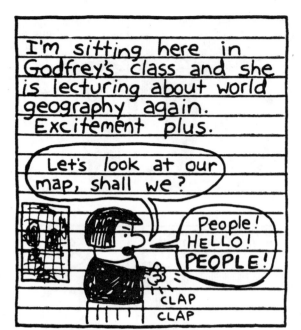

I'm sitting here in Godfrey's class and she is lecturing about world geography again. Excitement plus.

Let's look at our map, shall we?

People! HELLO! PEOPLE!

CLAP
CLAP

This stuff is so boring and useless it's unbelievable. Does she actually expect us to care?

Notice how Italy is in the shape of a boot!

As if there will EVER be a time in my life when I will need to know this stuff!

YAK YAK YAK

5
22

NATE, COME SHOW THE CLASS WHERE FIJI IS ON THE MAP, PLEASE.

POINK!

Peirce

**Awesome BIG NATE comics**

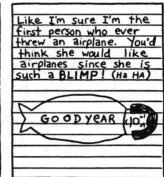

Rusty Sienna is back on t.v. for another season of "Oil Painting With Rusty," and guess what? Dad bought me my own paint set!

GA-BOING!

Of course I have always been Rusty's #1 fan, but now I will finally be more than just a spectator.

Let's paint, dag-nab it!

Now I can paint along with Rusty. Of all the presents Dad has ever given me, this is the greatest. My own paint set!

OOPS.

WHAT HAVE I DONE?

NOW, FRIENDS, AS YOU CAN SEE, I'M OPENING UP MY TUBE OF "SAP GREEN."

NOW I'M GOING TO APPLY THE PAINT IN A SERIES OF QUICK, VIGOROUS STROKES!

BRUSHA!
BRUSHA!
BRUSHA!

THERE! WE MADE A TREE! YOU'RE DOING GREAT!

OKAY, NOW LET'S PAINT A LITTLE CABIN....

BRUSH!
BRUSH!
BRUSH!

...AND NEXT TO THE CABIN ARE SOME LITTLE TREES PROVIDING SHADE...

BRUSH!
BRUSH!
BRUSH!

...AND STANDING IN THE SHADE IS A LITTLE DEER....

BRUSH!
BRUSH!
BRUSH!

WAIT UP!

...AND NEXT TO THE DEER IS A TINY LEPRECHAUN...

ADD MORE BABES!

I'VE MADE A DECISION, FRANCIS! I'VE DECIDED TO BECOME A "CHILD PRODIGY"!

YUP! I'LL BE ONE OF THOSE "BOY GENIUSES"! I'LL GRADUATE FROM COLLEGE BY THE TIME I'M FIFTEEN!

COME TO THINK OF IT, WHO NEEDS COLLEGE? I CAN PROBABLY MAKE A MILLION DOLLARS JUST BY SITTING AROUND BEING A CHILD PRODIGY!

TO BE A PRODIGY, YOU HAVE TO BE GOOD AT SOMETHING!

OH, YOU'RE A RIOT!

**Awesome BIG NATE comics**

**Panel 1:** WHAT MAKES YOU THINK **YOU** CAN BE A CHILD PRODIGY?
I'LL TELL YOU!

**Panel 2:** THE DICTIONARY DEFINES A PRODIGY AS "A PERSON, THING, OR ACT SO EXTRA-ORDINARY AS TO INSPIRE WONDER..."

**Panel 3:** "...SPECIFICALLY, A CHILD OF HIGHLY UNUSUAL TALENT OR GENIUS"!

**Panel 4:** NEED I SAY MORE?
PLEASE DON'T.

© 1992 United Feature Syndicate, Inc.

---

**Panel 5:** ✎ **CHILD PRODIGY!**
My plan to become a child prodigy is going great. Since I am so good at drawing and painting, I have decided to be an art prodigy.
Look!
No hands!

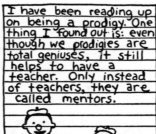

**Panel 6:** I have been reading up on being a prodigy. One thing I found out is: even though we prodigies are total geniuses, it still helps to have a teacher. Only instead of teachers, they are called mentors.

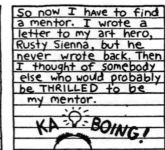

**Panel 7:** So now I have to find a mentor. I wrote a letter to my art hero, Rusty Sienna, but he never wrote back. Then I thought of somebody else who would probably be THRILLED to be my mentor.
KA-💡-BOING!

**Panel 8:** GREAT NEWS, MR. ROSA!
NOW WHAT?

© 1992 United Feature Syndicate, Inc.

---

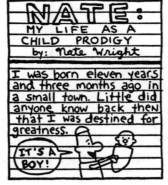

**Panel 9:** **NATE:** MY LIFE AS A CHILD PRODIGY by: Nate Wright
I was born eleven years and three months ago in a small town. Little did anyone know back then that I was destined for greatness.
IT'S A BOY!

**Panel 10:** At a very early age, I taught myself to draw. I practiced by making drawings of my sister Ellen. She was too stupid to appreciate my talents.
My nose is NOT that big!
"The truth hurts" is my motto!

**Panel 11:** The first person to recognize my genius was my 6th-grade art teacher, Mr. Rosa. He agreed to become my mentor even though he knew someday I would surpass him, art-wise.
I'll just bask in your glow!
Bask away!

**Panel 12:** I'M WRITING MY AUTOBIOGRAPHY **NOW**! ONCE I GET FAMOUS, I PROBABLY WON'T HAVE THE TIME!
GOOD THINKING.

© 1992 United Feature Syndicate, Inc.

---

**ADD MORE BABES!**

STANDARDIZED
# TEST!

A few weeks ago in school we took what is called a "vocational aptitude" test. Today we are getting the results.

Okay, people, break out those #2 pencils!

NO, you can't use a PEN! Did you hear me say "pen"?

The way the test works is: You answer all sorts of "multiple-choice" questions about your abilities and interests and stuff.

DANG these little ovals!

Then a computer analyzes the answers you gave and tells you what kind of a career you are going to have.

SOMETHING LUCRATIVE, I HOPE.

TELL ME ABOUT IT! MY ALLOWANCE IS PATHETIC!

MY STANDARDIZED TEST RESULTS SAY I'M GOOD AT "ANALYTICAL THINKING."

OOOooOH! NOW FOR MY RESULTS!

"YOU ARE A GENIUS."

WHAT IS THIS, SOME SORT OF CANDID CAMERA THING?

YES!

YOUR STANDARDIZED TEST RESULTS SAY YOU'RE A GENIUS?

IT'S A DIRTY JOB, BUT SOMEONE'S GOT TO DO IT!

IT IS KIND OF A BIG RESPONSIBILITY! THINK OF ALL THE GOOD YOU COULD DO! THE GREAT DEEDS YOU COULD ACCOMPLISH!

SO WHAT ARE YOU GOING TO DO FIRST?

QUIT SCHOOL, OF COURSE!

OF COURSE.

IF YOU WERE A GENIUS, FRANCIS, YOU WOULDN'T HAVE EVEN ASKED THAT QUESTION!

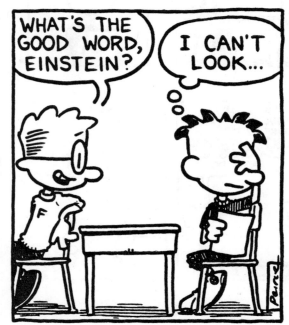

**Awesome BIG NATE comics**

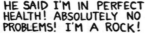

**ADD MORE BABES!**

☆ Mr. **ROSA!** ☆
Mr. Rosa is one of those teachers that, no matter when you go into his class-room, he is there.

Hey HEY HEY!

Sometimes if you go into his room after school, he is in there working on one of his own paintings. And if you are quiet, he will let you sit and watch.

DANG, I'm good!

That is what happened today. I was watching Mr. Rosa paint and then suddenly a question popped into my mind:

© 1991 United Feature Syndicate, Inc.

THIS GUY IS OUR ART TEACHER?

WHAT DO YOU THINK?

WHAT DO YOU THINK OF MY LATEST PAINTING, NATE?

I DON'T GET IT.

WELL, IT'S AN ABSTRACTION! IT'S PURELY AN EXERCISE IN COLOR AND FORM!

YEAH, BUT.... HOW DO YOU KNOW... I MEAN.... HOW CAN YOU TELL...?

© 1991 United Feature Syndicate, Inc.

.... WHAT IT MEANS?

NO, WHETHER YOU HAVE ANY ACTUAL TALENT.

THIS "ABSTRACT" STUFF IS OKAY, MR. ROSA, BUT CAN'T YOU DO ANY **REAL** ART?

SURE!

WHAT WOULD YOU LIKE ME TO DRAW?

A DOG!

THERE!

SAAAY! MR. ROSA! THAT'S NOT BAD!

© 1991 United Feature Syndicate, Inc.

OF COURSE, YOU'RE NO RUSTY SIENNA!

WELL, IT'S SOMETHING TO AIM FOR...

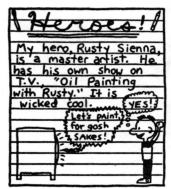

**Heroes!**

My hero, Rusty Sienna, is a master artist. He has his own show on T.V., "Oil Painting with Rusty." It is wicked cool.

*Let's paint, for gosh sakes!*

YES!

On each show, Rusty paints a masterpiece while giving useful secret art tips to the people watching at home.

*Rusty Rules!!*

Think of the brush as PART of your HAND!

His paintings are so much better than the stuff you see hanging in museums, but some people still don't like him. Dad, for example, is clueless about how awesome Rusty is.

?

BUT... ISN'T THAT THE SAME PAINTING HE DID **LAST** WEEK?

DAD, GET A **PULSE!** LAST WEEK'S PAINTING HAD **TWO** MOUNTAINS!

"OIL PAINTING WITH RUSTY" AGAIN?

YUP! MY FAVORITE SHOW!

I CONFESS I DON'T UNDER-STAND WHY....

WHY? BECAUSE RUSTY'S A **MASTER,** THAT'S WHY!

A **MASTER?** I DOUBT HE EVEN WENT TO ART SCHOOL!

**SURE** HE DID! SEE THAT FRAME ON THE WALL BE-HIND HIM? THAT'S HIS **DIPLOMA!**

I'VE NEVER SEEN A BLACK VELVET DIPLOMA BEFORE...

I SHOULD SAY **NOT!** THE "ART INSTITUTE OF P.O. BOX 73" DOESN'T ACCEPT JUST **ANYBODY!**

I **STILL** SAY ALL THIS GUY'S PAINTINGS LOOK ALIKE...

THAT'S NOT TRUE, DAD! YOU JUST DON'T KNOW RUSTY!

HE ALWAYS ADDS SOMETHING DIFFERENT TO EVERY PAINTING! YOU KNOW, FOR VARIETY! THAT'S WHAT MAKES HIM SUCH A GENIUS!

SEE WHAT I'M DOING HERE? BESIDE THIS REFLECTING POOL, I'M PAINTING A LITTLE BUNNY!

MY APOLOGIES TO THE MASTER...

LET'S PAINT A **LOT** OF BUNNIES! I'M IN A BUNNY MOOD!

**Awesome BIG NATE comics**

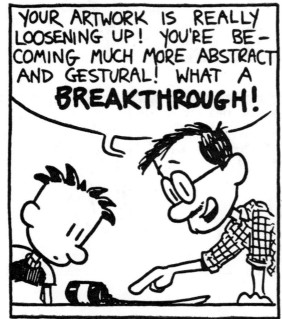

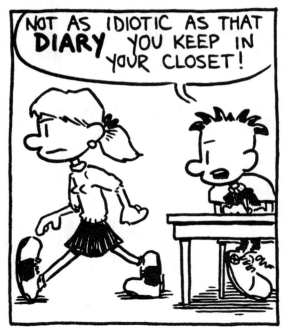

**Awesome BIG NATE comics**

**SPRING CLEANING!**

I finally make it to Spring Vacation and what happens? Dad decides we are going to do this mega-house cleaning! BOGUS!

A clean house is a HAPPY house!

I am like his cleaning slave. So far today I have vacuumed the whole house, cleaned the oven, scrubbed the tiles in the shower, and washed all the windows.

WORK!

Now I am sitting here in my room trying to rest before "Mr. Clean" strikes again. I just heard his voice, so I guess he has something else for me to do.

NATE!

HE PROBABLY WANTS ME TO POLISH HIS HEAD.

DAD! LOOK WHAT I FOUND WHILE I WAS CLEANING THE ATTIC! YOUR OLD "DISCO SUIT"!

HEE HEE! WERE YOU THE KING OF THE DISCOS, DAD?

OKAY, YOU CAN CUT THE SARCASM!

IT'S PROBABLY HARD FOR YOU TO IMAGINE, BUT I USED TO BE A VERY GOOD DANCER!

OH, I CAN IMAGINE IT!

Disco light →

THUMPA! THUMPA!

Disco beat

**DISCO FEVER!**

Hey babe what's your sign?

Get lost!

Do the hustle! Do the hustle!

Nice suit!

Thanks! 100% Polyester!

macho → chest hair

Wicked bell bottoms

THUMPA! KA-THUMPA!

I'll show all the babes some REAL smooth disco moves!

RIP!

Ha Ha Ha Ha

Ha Ha Ha Ha

I CALL THIS "THE ADVENTURES OF DAD, THE DISCO INFERNO!"

BACK TO WORK!

**Awesome BIG NATE comics**

GODFREY POSTED THE PAIRINGS FOR THE NEXT PROJECT.

AND **LOOK!** YOU AND I ARE ASSIGNED TO WORK TOGETHER!

WE'RE **PARTNERS!** AND YOU'RE ONE OF THE BIGGEST BRAINS IN SCHOOL! WHAT **LUCK!**

I'M PRACTICALLY **GUARAN-TEED** A GOOD GRADE! WHY, THIS COULD BE THE FIRST "A" OF MY CAREER!

...OR THE FIRST "D" OF MINE.

OKAY, OUR REPORT TOPIC IS "LOUISIANA."

OOOOOOH! "LAISSEZ LES BON TEMPS ROULLER!"

WE'VE GOT A FREE PERIOD! LET'S HIT THE LIBRARY!

THE LIBRARY?

OF COURSE! WE HAVE TO DO RESEARCH!

RESEARCH?

**YES!** DO YOU THINK THIS REPORT IS GOING TO WRITE **ITSELF?**

NO, I FIGURED **YOU'D** WRITE IT! I'LL HANDLE THE ILLUS-TRATIONS!

OKAY, I'VE COMPILED ALL THE SIGNIFICANT HISTORICAL EVENTS FOR OUR REPORT ON LOUISIANA...I'VE ARRANGED THEM IN CHRONOLOGICAL ORDER....AND I'VE WRITTEN BRIEF PROFILES OF ALL THE IMPORTANT SOCIAL AND POLITICAL FIGURES IN THE STATE'S HISTORY.

WHAT HAVE **YOU** DONE?

I'VE DRAWN A PICTURE OF A PELICAN!

WHY?

**WHY?** BECAUSE IT'S THE OFFICIAL STATE BIRD! COME **ON,** FRANCIS! DO I HAVE TO DO **ALL** THE WORK AROUND HERE?

I THINK IT'S GREAT THAT ART IS YOUR HOBBY, NATE!

HOBBY? ART IS MY LIFE!

WHEN DA VINCI PAINTED THE "MONA LISA," WAS THAT A HOBBY? WHEN MICHELANGELO PAINTED THE SISTINE CHAPEL, WAS THAT A HOBBY?

WHEN RUSTY SIENNA PAINTED "UNICORNS TOASTING MARSHMALLOWS IN PARADISE," WAS THAT A HOBBY?

ANOTHER ATTEMPT AT A FATHER-SON CHAT BITES THE DUST...

NO OFFENSE, DAD, BUT WHEN IT COMES TO ART, YOU'RE NOT EXACTLY THE SHARPEST TOOL IN THE SHED!

Yesterday Dad called Art my "hobby." He does not get it — Art is my LIFE!

draw draw

That is why Rusty Sienna is my total hero. He is a master artist, plus he has gotten rich doing it!

Not only does he have his own T.V. show, he also has his own books, instructional videos, art supplies, and hair care products!

Rusty Sienna Section

"HAIR CARE PRODUCTS?"

RUSTY'S PERM, DAD! IT REQUIRES CONSTANT MAINTENANCE!

HEY! I WAS WATCHING MY SOAP OPERA!

YOUR DUMB SOAP OPERA CAN WAIT, ELLEN.

CLIK!

IT'S 3:30! "OIL PAINTING WITH RUSTY" IS ON! I NEVER MISS IT! THAT'S WHAT WE'RE GOING TO WATCH!

DUE TO A LACK OF VIEWER SUPPORT, "OIL PAINTING WITH RUSTY" HAS BEEN CANCELLED.

OH. GOODY!

NO!

**ADD MORE BABES!**

**Panel 1:** SIGN MY PETITION, DAD! I'M ORGANIZING A CAMPAIGN TO GET "OIL PAINTING WITH RUSTY" BACK ON THE AIR!

**Panel 2:** LOOK AT ALL THOSE NAMES! THE TV STATION WILL HAVE A TOUGH TIME IGNORING **THIS!**

**Panel 3:** HMM.... THIS IS QUITE AN IMPRESSIVE LIST OF SIGNATURES, ALL RIGHT.

THE PEOPLE HAVE SPOKEN!

**Panel 4:** HOW INTERESTING THAT THEY'VE ALL SPOKEN IN YOUR HANDWRITING.

WELL, WHAT DO YOU EXPECT ME TO DO? WALK AROUND TO PEOPLE'S HOUSES?

© 1991 United Feature Syndicate, Inc.

---

**Panel 5:**
Dear T.V. Executive:

Are you the bonehead who cancelled "Oil Painting with Rusty"? If so, you should be shot. How could you get rid of the greatest show in T.V. history and replace it with "Glenda's Green Garden"? You are a moron. I hate your guts.

**Panel 6:**
Rusty brings joy to millions of faithful viewers. Apparently you are just too clueless to understand that the man is an artistic genius. You probably wouldn't know a great work of art if you tripped over one. How did you ever get to be a T.V. executive?

**Panel 7:**
I hope reading this letter (if you can read) makes you realize the error of your ways. Wake up and put Rusty back on the air or you will regret the day you were ever born. ACT NOW OR ELSE!!!

P.S.- I know where you live.

Sincerely,
Nate Wright

**Panel 8:** TELL YOU WHAT, SON.... LEAVE THIS WITH ME AND **I'LL** MAIL IT FOR YOU!

DO YOU LIKE THE SKULL AND CROSSBONES I DREW UNDERNEATH MY SIGNATURE?

© 1991 United Feature Syndicate, Inc.

---

**Panel 9:** DAD! GUESS WHAT? THE TV STATION PUT "OIL PAINTING WITH RUSTY" BACK ON THE AIR!

**Panel 10:** I **KNEW** THAT LETTER I WROTE WOULD DO THE TRICK!

WELL, I IMAGINE THE STATION RECEIVED **LOTS** OF LETTERS....

**Panel 11:** YEAH, BUT IT WAS **MINE** THAT MADE THE DIFFERENCE! I'M **CERTAIN** OF IT!

**Panel 12:** IT MUST BE NICE TO BE THAT CERTAIN OF **ANYTHING**....

© 1991 United Feature Syndicate, Inc.

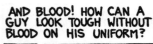

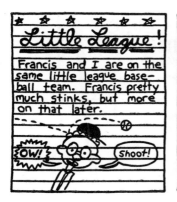

**Little League!**

Francis and I are on the same little league baseball team. Francis pretty much stinks, but more on that later.

OW! ... Shoot!

Our team has a sponsor called "Joe's Pizza." So that is what our uniforms say on them.

JOE'S PIZZA

Other teams have cool names like the Giants, Eagles, and Hawks, and we are called Joe's Pizza. It is not fair.

COME ON, PIZZAS!

LOOK! THE OTHER TEAM IS LAUGHING AT US!

WHAT'S THE MATTER? YOU'VE WALKED FOUR GUYS IN A ROW!

IT'S OUR TEAM NAME! IT'S RUINING MY CONCENTRATION!

I CAN'T PITCH WHILE EVERYBODY'S YELLING "LET'S GO, PIZZAS!" IT'S RIDICULOUS!

IT MAKES ME FEEL SO.... SO....

HUNGRY?

STARVING! MY PRE-GAME TWINKIE HAS WORN OFF COMPLETELY!

SIGH..... ANOTHER LOSS...

2!...4!...6!...8! WHO DO WE APPRECIATE? JOE'S PIZZA! JOE'S PIZZA! YAAAAAY!

...AND HOLD THE ANCHOVIES!

HA HA HA HA HA HA HA HA HA

WISE GUYS...

99

ADD MORE BABES!

THAT MR. ROSA IS A RIOT!

I ASKED HIM WHAT HE'S GOING TO DO ON HIS SUMMER VACATION, AND HE SAID "WORK!"

...AND WHEN I ASKED HIM WHY, HE SAID "BECAUSE I CAN'T SURVIVE ON MY TEACHER'S SALARY!" HA HA HA HA HA! OH HO HO HO HO!

THAT MR. ROSA IS A RIOT!

---

NOW WHAT ARE YOU WRITING IN THAT DUMB BOOK?

A NOVEL.

IT'S THE STORY OF A WACKY MOTHER SUPERIOR WHO'S ALSO THE PILOT OF A BOEING 747! SHE FLIES AROUND THE COUNTRY DOING GOOD DEEDS!

I CALL IT "NUN OF THE ABOVE!"

NOBODY APPRECIATES LITERARY HUMOR...

---

WHAT ARE YOU DRAWING, NATE?

A COMIC STRIP! IT'S CALLED "DINNER WITH DAD!"

SEE? IN THIS PANEL, YOU'RE COOKING DINNER... THEN, IN THIS PANEL, WE'RE EATING DINNER...

...AND IN THIS PANEL, YOU'RE GIVING ME A BIG HUG! WHY, THAT'S VERY SWEET, NATE!

I HAD NO IDEA YOU WERE SO SENTIMENTAL!

I'M NOT! THAT'S THE "HEIMLICH MANEUVER"!

**LAST DAY OF SCHOOL!**

☆ ☆ ☆ ☆ ☆ ☆ ☆ ☆

After 179 days of torture, the last day of school is finally here! AWESOME!!

This is one day I don't mind going to school because there are no tests or anything. Everybody just wants vacation to start.

Today we don't even have to bring our books with us!

But that does not mean we go to school empty-handed!

THANK-YOU GIFTS FOR ALL MY TEACHERS. WHAT'S IN **YOUR** BAG?

TWO DOZEN EGGS AND A CHERRY BOMB!

© 1991 United Feature Syndicate, Inc.

I WANTED TO WISH YOU A HAPPY SUMMER, MR. ROSA!

THANK YOU, NATE! SAME TO YOU!

I ALSO WANTED TO LET YOU KNOW THERE'S NO HARD FEELINGS!

HARD FEELINGS? ABOUT WHAT?

DON'T ACT INNOCENT, MR. ROSA! I UNDERSTAND WHY YOU DIDN'T INCLUDE MY FINAL PROJECT IN THE "STUDENT ARTWORK" EXHIBIT!

FINAL PROJECT?...

© 1991 United Feature Syndicate, Inc.

AH, YES..... "DR. CESSPOOL REMOVES HIS OWN TONSILS".

DIDN'T WANT ME SHOWING UP THE LESS TALENTED STUDENTS, EH?

OKAY, I FINISHED SIGNING YOUR YEARBOOK!

I FINISHED YOURS TOO! HERE!

Nate- You are the best buddy a guy could have. Plus, you are an awesome artist! We're going to have a great summer!

Your pal, Francis

Francis- You still owe me thirty-five cents for that twinkie you stole from me in February. Are you going to pay up or **WHAT??**  Nate

© 1991 United Feature Syndicate, Inc.

**GEE!** HOW **TOUCH-ING!**

HEY, I DIDN'T CHARGE YOU INTEREST, DID I? **DID** I?

**Awesome BIG NATE comics**

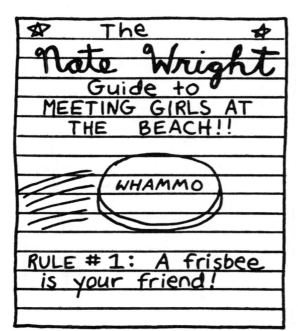

**Awesome BIG NATE comics**

**ADD MORE BABES!**

NATE, WHAT ARE YOU DOING HERE?

I CAME TO WATCH YOU IN ACTION!

YOU CAN'T JUST STAND HERE AT THE COUNTER! YOU HAVE TO ORDER SOMETHING!

OKAY! I'LL TAKE A "DOUBLE DILLY DELUXE"!

THAT'LL BE $2.39.

WHA...? YOU'RE CHARGING ME FOR IT? BUT I'M YOUR BROTHER!!

THANK YOU FOR THE REMINDER.

DANG! JUST WHEN I THOUGHT BEING RELATED TO YOU WAS FINALLY GOING TO PAY OFF!

OKAY, NATE, YOU'VE BUGGED ME ENOUGH! I GAVE YOU YOUR BURGER! NOW GET OUT OF HERE!

YOU'LL GET ME IN TROUBLE IF YOU JUST HANG AROUND! HIT THE ROAD! GET LOST! SCRAM! SCAT! VAMOOSE!

WELL? WHAT ARE YOU WAITING FOR?

YOU DIDN'T SAY "COME AGAIN!"

BEAT IT!

ELLEN'S JOB!!

Today I went down to "Dilly Burger" because it was Ellen's first day of working there. But did she give me any free food? I think NOT!

Hey! Hey! HEY!

What do YOU want?

She has the easiest job I've ever seen. All she does is stand behind a counter all day. And they actually PAY her for it!

La LA LA dum de dum...♪ Hello gorgeous!

SLAM!

I CAN'T BELIEVE I'M ONLY GETTING MINIMUM WAGE....

**Awesome BIG NATE comics**

By day, their identities are **CHUCK UPLEY**, multi-billionaire man-about-town, and *NED TEDSON*, his pimply-faced ward!

Polo, anyone?
Heck yes, Chuck!

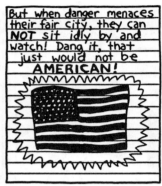

But when danger menaces their fair city, they can **NOT** sit idly by and watch! Dang it, that just would not be AMERICAN!

So they don their costumes and assume their SECRET IDENTITIES! They BECOME...

"KIT AND KABOODLE, MASTER CRIME-FIGHTERS"?

READ ON, DAD!

© 1991 United Feature Syndicate, Inc.

7-22

---

The Adventures of **KIT** and **KABOODLE**!

What's that, Chief? You say the evil BUCKETHEAD is on the loose?

E-GAD! To the KIT-MOBILE!

KABOODLE

KIT

Hey! What happened to the KIT-MOBILE?

It's in the shop! We'll have to make do with this powder-blue 1972 Dodge "Swinger!"

Zounds! How embarrassing! What if some of my friends from school see me riding in this thing?

7 23

Kaboodle, you MEAT-HEAD! None of your friends from school know your SECRET IDENTITY!

Oh.... Right!

continued!

© 1991 United Feature Syndicate, Inc.

---

**MIDNIGHT!** Kit and Kaboodle are staking out the warehouse headquarters of the evil BUCKETHEAD!

That fiendish fiend!

"Fiendish fiend?"

BUCKETHEAD and his goons are over there, but I can't see what they're up to!

7 29

K

Here, Kit! I'll turn on the lights!

CLICK!

NO!

Hey! Look!

© 1991 United Feature Syndicate, Inc.

You idgit.

Whoops.

continued!

---

**ADD MORE BABES!**

So, Kit, you thought you could foil me! But I've **WON**! In thirty seconds this giant saw will cut you in **HALF**!

**GOODBYE**, Kit and Kaboodle! Goodbye **FOREVER**! WA HA HA HA HA HA HA HA!

RRRRR

7 25

E-GAD! What a dastardly villain!

You said it!

RRRRR!

Why do they call him "Buckethead?"

RRRRR!

continued!

WOW! KIT AND KABOODLE ARE ABOUT TO BE CUT IN HALF BY A GIANT SAW! HOW WILL YOU GET THEM OUT OF THIS ONE?

KEEP READING, DAD!

We're doomed!

No we're not, chum!

RRRR

**TONG!**

Thank Heavens for that steel plate in my head!

Boy! I'LL say!

YOU'RE A GENIUS.

I KNOW.

7 26

We've done it again, Kaboodle! The evil **BUCKETHEAD** is behind bars!

Yes, Kit! We can go back to being CHUCK UPLEY and his ward, NED TEDSON!

Not so fast, chum! Look at **THAT**!!

Zounds!

**THE END**

A GREAT CARTOONIST ALWAYS LEAVES HIS READERS WANTING MORE!

7 27

© 1991 United Feature Syndicate, Inc.

# WHY SETTLE FOR LESS WHEN YOU CAN HAVE IT ALL?

## COLLECTIONS OF YOUR FAVORITE COMIC STRIPS ...

_____ ARE WE THERE YET?
A Frank & Ernest History of the World  $5.95
_____ ASSEMBLE THE HYENAS
A Frank & Ernest Book of Puns  $6.95
_____ CYBERPUNKTREK
A Robotman Collection  $6.95
_____ DAD, I'M AN ELVIS IMPERSONATOR
 A Drabble Book  $6.95
_____ STEEL-BELTED GRIMMY
A Mother Goose & Grimm Book  $5.95
_____ 4-WHEEL GRIMMY
Another Mother Goose & Grimm Book  $5.95
_____ GRIMMY COME HOME
More Mother Goose & Grimm  $6.95
Mother Goose & Grimm's
_____ NIGHT OF THE LIVING VACUUM  $8.95

_____ TOTAL BOOKS (add $1.50 per book for
postage & handling)

Please rush me the above titles. I've enclosed a check or money order for _____ made out to Pharos Books.

Name _____
Address_____
City_____ State_____ Zip_____

Send completed form and payment to Pharos Books, Sales Dept., 200 Park Avenue, New York, NY 10166